A Girl's Room
Marjun Syderbø Kjelnæs

A Girl's Room

Marjun Syderbø Kjelnæs

Translated by
Matthew Landrum and Rakul Í Gerðinum

© 2024 Marjun Syderbø Kjelnaes

Funded, in part, by a grant from Farlit,
Faroe Islands

Originally published in Faroese as
Gentukamarid by Ungu Føroyar, 2022

ISBN 979-8-9884732-4-4

IPI Press books are distributed in North
America by Casemate Publishers and in
the rest of the world by Oxbow Books.

www.ipolari.com

A Girl's Room
An Existential Horror Comedy

Marjun Syderbø Kjelnæs

translated by Matthew Landrum
and Rannvá H. Glerfoss

Dramatis Personae

Woman
Phantom
Mother
Attendant

Act 1
Scene 1

Setting: A room with paisley wallpaper and a fireplace. A movable partition stands against a chimney near a made bed. There's a model sailing ship on a dresser and a desk covered in knick-knacks. On the desk sits a reading lamp, a mirror, and a pink journal. On the wall hangs a framed print of two children crossing a bridge, a guardian angel hovers over them. A white boombox sits on the windowsill.

"Islands in the Stream" by Dolly Parton and Kenny Rogers is playing.

Curtain rises: A beanbag stirs, Phantom rises to its feet.

Phantom *stretches stiff joints, as if it has been cramped up for a long while. It looks contentedly around then walks a turn about the room nodding at the familiar objects. It turns off the music, squats by the dresser and pulls out a drawer. Shakes head, dumps out a heap of disassembled dolls onto the floor, and sits down to assemble them.*

So you're coming home. After all this time. I can feel it. The signs are all here. Daddy has aired out the room. Mom made your bed. Everything's ready.

Sits down at the vanity.

But what are you running from? Coming back home (to hide), here of all places? What good could that possibly do?

Furrows brow and hides its face behind its hands.

BOO!

Okay. Okay. Maybe I get it. Sometimes you need to come home again, to disappear for a while — from the world, from yourself. Still... here?
Laughs hysterically.

Your girlhood room as a place to hide. Just think of it! This place is everything you once were, everything you wanted to be. Oh, little one...

Your girlhood room as a lifeboat. Ridiculous! Sweet but naive.

Your girlhood room as a trench. That's more like it.

Holds a doll in each hand, making them fight, until one of them loses the fight and its head.

You all remember the nursery rhyme don't you? The one about the magical clock that ran backwards and the girl who wouldn't shut up and how the clock's hands tangled in her hair.

Talk, talk.
Tick, tock.
Talk, talk.
Tick, tock.
When the clock struck four,

there were screams and gore.
At the stroke of midnight,
her head took flight.

Alright. Alright. Don't worry. I'll be nice when she gets here.

Carefully puts the dolls back into the drawer, turns on the music,
and puts on some pajamas, lays down on the bed,
then quickly sits back up and remains in place.

Scene Two

Curtain rises. The room is darkening.
Light shines on Woman as she walks in
talking on the phone.
She turns off the music.

Woman
No. That won't work.

Listens.

We've tried that before.

Listens.

No. Listen. Listen to me. We tried it and it didn't work. She's trying. She lays down and falls asleep.

Listens.

No!

If you do that she'll wake up and she won't know where she is and then she'll scream and wake the whole house.

Listens.

Right. And you'll have to stay up with her until she stops crying and she'll be so distraught and disappointed and the whole next day will be shot.

Because she'll be exhausted.

Listens.

Yes. Actually it is like that. We both know it.

Listens while pacing around the room.

I don't give a damn about your stag party. This is our daughter we're talking about.

Listens.

No. I can't come.

Listens.

Because I can't. The ferry left hours ago. What do you want me to do, swim?

Listens.

Are you kidding me? I'm not boycotting you. Excuse me for not coming to your wedding to be some stand-in nanny for our child. Maybe you need an extra bridesmaid while we're at it?

Hello.

Fucking hell.

> **Woman** *stomps around and throws the phone down.*
> *While she's been on the phone a change has come over the room.*
> *It's brighter.* **Phantom** *watches as* **Woman** *changes*
> *into the pajamas laid out for her on the bed,*

*a matching set to the ones **Phantom** is wearing.*
Woman lies down on the bed then sits up
*next to **Phantom** who is already sitting there.*
She speaks to the seemingly empty room.

Ugh. This is unreal!

Phantom
I'm gonna stop you right there.

Woman
I could just scream.

Phantom
Naturally.

Woman
Or cry.

Phantom
Let it out.

Woman
This is all so pathetic. Unreal.

Phantom
Now you're getting things a bit mixed up.

Woman
What do you want from me? Why are you here?

Phantom
Tonight, I'll swim through the cold ocean currents and find my
way to your daughter before she wakes alone in a strange house.

Woman *to* *Phantom.*

Yes.

Phantom

I'll take her in my arms ever so gently.

Woman

Yes!

Phantom

And carry her out beneath the shining stars, and she'll dream that every possibility is twinkling up there in the sky above her.

Woman

Will you really? Please?

Phantom

No!

*Gets up and starts mincing around the room
speaking in a sarcastic tone.*

Tomorrow I'll put on a flowing white dress and long silk stockings

Sets a jeweled diadem on their head.

Woman *puts her hand over her ears.*

Phantom

And I'll pull a blue garter all the way up my thigh and hold on ever so tightly to a sweet-smelling bouquet.

Woman

Shut up!

Phantom
"Do you take this man to be…"

Woman *stands up and shouts in **Phantom**'s face.*
This can't be real!

Phantom
Okay, I need to make you aware of three points:
1. You are here of your own free will.
2. You can't just make claims without explaining yourself.
3. I'm only a projection of your unconscious desires.

I know this is hard.

Woman
Who… what are you?

Phantom
I am the silkworm that eats through the fabric of your dreams.

Woman
You can't be real. This is so pathetic.

Phantom
I'm going to stop you right there.

Phantom rolls the partition out in front of them,
puts on scrubs and presses a remote. The partition becomes
an x-ray screen. Inside Woman's skeleton, the sloping ceiling
of the room is visible. Phantom pulls out
an extendable pointer and puts on a scientific tone,
pointing and explaining.

A girl's room exists: wallpaper and silence and a hundred little things.

It may appear to be a fossil or an artifact, maybe one that belongs in a glass display on sexual evolution.

Or maybe it's a storage room, a warehouse of irrelevant things, a museum no one would ever buy a ticket to.

   Woman *sits down on bed.*
This is messed up.

   Phantom
Yes.

     Continuing in academic voice.

The room is outdated.

Not quite a curiosity — not yet.

It's only out of fashion.

A golden cage.

A cheese bell.

From its depths, you can hear voices — the Madonna and the whore, the angelic girl, the she-devil.

Here we have framed scripture. And a faded picture of children and their guardian angel.

A made bed.

A journal half full of poetry.

It's too early to say if this is significant, impossible to say, but unreal it is not. The girlhood room exists, damn it!

> *The partition rolls away. Phantom puts on latex gloves*
> *and opens a drawer, taking out a doll.*
> *Puts it on the desk and lights the lamp*
> *and leans over the doll like a pathologist.*

Dolls exist too: combed, swaddled, dissected, stuck with pins until they look like a hedgehog while girls cackle in that evil way only voodoo priestesses can pull off.

> *Laughs.*

Woman *cries softly.*

Phantom
I know. I know.

Woman *screams.*

Phantom
Let it all out.

Woman *lies down.*

Phantom *tucks Woman in.*

Woman
Do you think she'll wake up?

Phantom
Hush now.

Woman
Will they hear her cry out?

Phantom *sings.*
"The moment I wake up, before I put on my make-up, I say a little prayer for you."

Woman *Stands up and rummages through a drawer.*

Phantom
"And while I'm combing my hair now, and wonder what dress to wear now, I say a little prayer for you…"

Woman
Shut up!

Phantom
Okay. Okay. Perhaps a story instead?

Puts a pipe in its mouth, sits down, and crosses its legs.

Once upon a time… Once upon a time there was a girl named Agnes Louise. She was a sweet girl, hardworking, gentle, plain but not ugly. She did everything that was asked of her — laundry, cooking, minding the little ones. And, since this was a long time ago, also milking the cows, carrying peat, drying fish, mucking out the stalls, that sort of thing.

But… but, but, but, our Agnes Louise was different, special. She kept growing long after the other girls in the village stopped. Five feet. Six feet. Seven feet. She grew taller than all the men in the village, taller, much taller. The way Agnes grew — it was grotesque. She grew so much that her poor Mother wouldn't let her outside. You can only imagine how hard it was for her!

I mean, houses were small back then. Think of Agnes Louise crouched beneath the rafters.

> **Woman** *puts on a pink kimono that's too small and a pair of slipper that don't fit any more.*
Stop!

Phantom
I'm not done yet. This is a good story.

Woman
None of this is real.

Phantom
We've been over this. Remember the three points — free will, explain your claims, manifestation of unconscious desire. Blah. Blah.

Woman
This is all so pathetic.

Phantom
Yes, pathos. That's what I was getting to. Nothing is as pathetic as a girl's room. But on the other hand…

> **Woman** *turns on the boombox. "Islands in the Stream" plays again. Turns up the volume and sings along. Takes the doll off of the autopsy table, hugs it to her as she dances.*

> **Phantom** *tries to keep talking, yells with a preacher's voice*
Maybe that's the case. But at the same time, nothing's as holy as a girl's room. It's all wound up with blood and confessions and anxieties.

"If a Woman conceives and bears a child, she shall be unclean for seven days, as many days as when she is menstruating and blood flows from her nakedness, and anyone who touches her shall be unclean until evening. The man shall be innocent, but the Woman shall pay for her misdeed."

Knocking at the door.

Woman *turns off the music. The oil burner clanks.*
Who is it?

Mother
Just me, honey. Is everything alright in there?

Woman
Yes, mom. Just listening to my old Kenny and Dolly CD.

Mother
Okay. We're heading to bed. Your father's already asleep.

Woman
Sorry. I'll keep it down.

Mother
Goodnight, sweetheart.

Woman
Goodnight, mom.

Phantom *Imitating.*
Goodnight, sweetheart.

Woman
You. Shut up. Now.

Scene Three

Curtain rises: The oil burner hums. Woman drifts around the room. Phantom follows her imitating her actions like a caricaturist. Woman shoves Phantom away and sits down at the desk and opens the journal. She begins writing, pausing occasionally until stopping completely.

Phantom *shrugs and rummages through a dresser drawer, pulling out various items of clothing, all the while humming "I Say a Little Prayer for You".*

Oh, look at this one!

Pulls out a dress.

Woman *doesn't look up, puts a finger to lips*

Phantom *whispering*
And this one.

Pulls out a scarf.

Woman *shakes her head*

Phantom
And this one.

Admires a woolen hat.

Woman *puts down her pencil and folds her hands,*
as in prayer.

Phantom *offended.*
I'm not some evil spirit, you know!

Woman *shuts eyes.*

Phantom
I'm not evil!

Woman *sighs.*

Phantom
Yoohoo! Hello.

Woman
Shh.

Phantom *whispers again.*
Look at these!

Waves a pair of leg warmers around.

Woman *looks up and smiles.*

Phantom
What were you thinking!?

Hands Woman one of the leg warmers.

Woman
It was the 80's.

Puts it on.

Phantom

And?

Hands her the other one.
"Bette Davis Eyes" by Kim Carnes is heard playing,
louder and louder.

Woman

The music.

Puts it on.

Phantom

And?

Hands her more and more clothing.

Woman

The lights.

Dances, putting on the clothing as they are handed to her.

Phantom

And?

Woman

There were butterflies in my stomach

Phantom

And?

Woman

My head spun.

Phantom
And?

Woman
Everything was possible.

Phantom
And?

Woman
Nothing was out of reach.

Phantom
And?

Woman
I jumped.

Phantom
And?

Woman
I floated in thin air.

Phantom
And?

Woman *is now tangled up in so many pieces of clothing, her mouth is hidden. She can no longer stand up straight and falls onto the floor. The music stops.*

Phantom
Whoopsie daisy!

Starts helping Woman to her feet,
but ends up tying her up even tighter.
The oil burner stops.
The cell phone rings. Phantom picks it up.

Woman *lays on the floor while violently shaking her head no. Tries escaping while kicking at Phantom.*

Phantom *speaks in an overly friendly manner, while dodging the kicks.*

Yes, hello!

Listens.

Yes, this is her phone.

Listens.

Unfortunately, she's a bit tied up at the moment.

Listens.

Oh, come on, nothing like that.

Listens.

Yes, I can take a message.

Furrows brow.

I see…

Listens.

I see…

Listens.

Well, you know what, old boy, I have a message for you too.

I an officious voice.

In a girl's room one can hear the silence between the stars. And when the sun shines, the universe vibrates in the dust.

Between sleep and wakefulness, seething magma bubbles, and seeps into the unconscious. The certainty of a Mother of all.

A Woman is a globe with a fetus inside, with milk inside. A labyrinth of desire.

The moon pulls at her body fluids, sparkles in her warm puddles, glistens in her salty streams.

A girl's room is the quietest place on earth.

From far off, you can faintly catch the tolling of a clock, hear how years slice off of minutes.

A little girl closes her eyes, a Woman opens them. Here daylight and dusk are a tangle of time.

Hours move in a circular motion, inwards. Always inwards.

Hello! Hello?

Scornfully looks at the phone and puts it down.

Bachelor party.

Woman *gives up trying to escape and lies motionless on the floor.*

Phantom *leafs through the poetry in the journal and shakes head. Lies down on the bed with a hand under its chin and looks at Woman.*

There was a girl who visited you. She slept on the floor, right here. Your cousin, I think. Do you remember? Skinny, pale, a flair for horror.

"When you wake up tomorrow, Jesus will have come back," she whispered. Remember? Her voice creaked like a cellar door.

She was a little older than you and would have known all about when a savior might be expected to turn up and who they might save.

"You'll look for us and won't find anyone. You'll call and call and no one will answer you."

And then she fell asleep, and you were alone with your heart which beat and beat and beat.

The flowers on the wallpaper withered that night.

Their petals fell onto your face. And you were a little dead princess.

Woman *begins writhing to get free again.*

Phantom
Oh dear! I forgot you were there.

Starts to free her. Then stops.

Phantom
Okay, I am aware this deviates a bit from point one — free will and all that — but, but, but this is your own fault really. You provoked me with all that flimflam.

Makes a sign of the cross and folds hands as in prayer.

Woman *begins to struggle again.*

Phantom
Hey, now! Remember point three? I am in essence a manifestation of your unconscious desires. So you really can't blame me for this situation, eh?

Woman *manages a hoarse cry.*

Phantom
Shh. Daddy's asleep, remember?

Woman *hisses menacingly.*

Phantom
Do you want me to let you go?

Woman *stares back angrily.*

Phantom
Well, do you?

Woman *nods.*

Phantom
Then you have to promise one thing. Can you do that?

Woman *shakes her head, shrugs, then nods.*

Phantom
Good – well then, this might sound like a fairy tale, but it isn't, or, rather, it has some fairytale-like elements, but essentially it's — what's the right term — a therapeutic exercise. It builds character.

Woman *growing impatient.*

Phantom

Oh right. Sorry, I'll get to the point. Quickly – again, three things: beginning, middle, end. You talk. I listen. And the subject is…

> *Gets up and walks around, puts on a cap*
> *and a double-buttoned army jacket.*
> *Looks into the diary again,*
> *smiles and inclines head sideways.*

Hmm… Guilt, shame, here we go — fear! The one and only — that classic, old tormenter.

But you have to tell the whole story. No cheating. You know, I love a good story. And so I ask you: Do you cross your heart and hope to die and swear you'll tell me your deepest fear if I let you go?

Do you?

Woman *can't speak.*

Phantom
Oops! My bad.

Loosens the tangle of clothes until Woman can speak.

Woman
This is so pathetic.

Phantom
Beep. Wrong answer.

Ties Woman up again.
Woman struggles.
As they tussle, Phantom continues speaking.

I tried to skirt around this before but you are correct: this is
pathetic, yes, but on the other hand, maybe nothing is as grand as
a girlhood room?

Puts on a sequined quiz master jacket.

Is there strength in every little thing we find here?

Beeep!

Thousands of years of oppression, yet you still love flowers, love
them enough to actually like flowered wallpaper?

Beeep!

Sitting there, rocking the doll, which one day will be a living
child — your own.

Are you getting used to being a pair of arms, a safe harbor, a
resting place?

Beep!

No-no, a girl's room is a boot camp, this is where we train to fight:

Guerilla girl partisans forever!

A doll in your arms and a flower in your thoughts.

From here we go forth to face a world of hatred and violence.

Marching forward. Damn the torpedoes!

Long live the revolution!

> *Gets louder, eventually shouting.*

Viva la girl's room!

> *Phantom has now roughed Woman up
> so badly she's no longer moving.*

Oh, damn it… hey, you, wake up, my dear!

> *A knock sounds at the door.*

Mother
Is everything alright in there, sweetheart?

> **Phantom** *Panicked, turns off the music. Puts on a bright tone of voice.*

Just listening to Dolly and Kenny!

Mother
That's not what it sounded like.

Phantom
Sorry. It won't happen again.

Mother
But… Oh, okay. Goodnight, dear.

Phantom
Goodnight, mom

Woman *imitating.*
Goodnight, mom

Phantom
Holy shit! Are you okay?

Woman
What do you care? That's why you're here, right? To glory in the fact that I'm not okay?

Phantom
No, no, no — I'm not on nobody's side. Neither for or against.

Woman
So what? You're just here to ridicule me with all this nonsense about me and this room?

Phantom
Look — you came home to your childhood room and I was here to greet you. Alright, maybe I've been a tad dramatic. But what is life without a stage, where we poor players strut and fret our hour, and worry and lose our patience?

Woman
I'm trapped.

Phantom
Yes, I understand what you mean. It is quite cramped, and the view isn't much to write home about either. If you ask me, I actually think it's rather oppressive.

Woman
I can't move.

Phantom
You're right. Not really much head room in here.

Now that you mention it, that's kinda how it was for Agnes Louise. I mean, in the end there wasn't any room for her in the house, and in the middle of the night they had to take the door jamb off to shove her into the courtyard.

They say that when Agnes Louise stood up and stretched her sore back that night, she was as tall as the ball of the flagpole in front of the town church. Her Mother wept, her father crossed himself, and all her younger siblings ran around her, screaming.

Clambers onto the bed, then jumps to the chair,
then the table, then the dresser, while undressing.

Her clothes were ragged and torn. Everyone hid their eyes, because so much skin was showing. Agnes Louise was huge and horrible and almost naked!

Woman
Hey!

Phantom

When they recovered from their shock, the girl was on her way down the hill, and I'll tell you: she went fast. With every giant step she moved further and further away.

"Where are you going?!" yelled her Mother.

But Agnes Louise never turned around. She just walked and walked, and grew and grew… until she completely vanished from sight.

Woman

I am literally tied up!

Phantom

Oh dear, that's right. I'll let you go but…

Woman

Okay. Okay. I swear.

Phantom

And.

Woman

Cross my heart.

Phantom

And.

Woman

Hope to die.

Phantom

That?

Woman

That what?

Phantom *puts on a beret and puts a cigarette in a long holder in its mouth.*

Ho hum, you know, sometimes people duck out on their promises. Maybe I wasn't completely clear what the agreement was about, so unfortunately I have to make sure we're on the same page.

Woman

What do you want from me?

Phantom

Dear God, my dear, you have to tell me a story with three parts — beginning, middle, and end — that reveals your deepest fear. Furthermore, you must do it in a way that suits the dignity of your girlhood room. C'est tout!

Woman

Then you'll leave me in peace?

Phantom

Now you're just being mean. We'll be at peace together!

Woman

Fine!

Phantom *looks at her imploringly.*

Woman

I will tell you a story — beginning, middle, and end — that reveals my deepest fear in a way that suits the dignity of my girlhood room.

Phantom
Voila!

You won't regret this!

Puts on a solemn expression and gesticulates.

Your girlhood room is the place you first caught the scent of the world.

It was a haven and prison, a spotlit stage where all your dreams came to life.

But most of all, it was a waiting room because, when it came right down to it, you knew nothing about the world you longed for. This is where you dreamed your most beautiful dreams.

Everything was steeped in innocence then. And your parents, they loved you so very deeply, so it was obvious, even then, that you would never do anything original, anything of consequence.

You were just an ordinary girl in an ordinary room.

Woman
Let me go.

Phantom
Oh, right! Sorry.

Releases her.

Scene Four

Curtain rises: The oil burner hums.
Woman shakes with rage as she paces the room.
She walks to the chimney, finds a bottle behind it
and wipes off the dust.
She turns on "Bohemian Rhapsody"
and twists off the cap.

Phantom
Seriously?

Woman *takes a swig.*

Phantom
That's basically cheating.

Woman
You didn't say anything about drinking.

Phantom
Alright, well… nevermind. But if this affects the quality of the story, no way does this count as a mitigating circumstance. Just saying!

Woman *drinks without answering.*

Phantom
Lovely, lovely. So dark and tortured. A Woman tormented.

Enough, thank you!

Cut!

And go.

Woman *sings along.*

Phantom
Get going already!

Woman *laughs mockingly, stands up and sings along using a hairbrush as a microphone.*

Phantom *hangs head and smiles, walks behind the partitioned wall, comes back out in Dolly drag with a wig and sparkly dress, takes the hairbrush from Woman. The music fades out.*

Woman *sits down and takes a drink.*

Phantom *stands behind Woman and begins to brush her hair, speaking in a gossipy tone, eyes wide.*

Did you know that in olden days there was a drink that could reveal whether or not a Woman had been unfaithful? You just took a handful of dust from the floor of the tabernacle and mixed it with water and had the Woman under suspicion drink it. And while she drank, the high priest said, "this water, cursed, will go down into your bowels, so that your abdomen swells, and your loins will waste away, if you speak untrue!" And the Woman answered — do you know what she answered?

Woman *hesitates her drinking, and shakes her head.*

Phantom *gesticulates arms and speaks with an American accent.*

"Amen, and amen!" she answered. And then, then verily she drank. Drank and drank.

Woman *looks at the bottle in her hand and puts it down.*

Phantom
But of course, this was in the old days, in the beginning of time, long before poor Agnes Louise's time.

She also fell victim to the bottle, by the by; Agnes Louise – or to the barrel, you might technically say. She found a cavern far away from her home. And I kid you not, at night she would walk about laying waste to the surrounding villages, destroying everything in her path, from hunger or sorrow, or both. I don't really know.

The only thing they could do, the villagers, I mean, was to drug her, so they got together and carried keg after keg to her, barrel after barrel, as if she was an angry idol they worshiped.

Poor abnormally large Agnes Louise.

Woman
Oh, boohoo. That has nothing to do with me.

Takes a sip.

Phantom *grabs Woman by the hair, which is now brushed back into a pony-tail, and snatches the bottle from her. Phantom breaks it on the edge of the table, and pushes the sharp edge into Woman's face, menacingly.*

Maybe you think I'm messing around? That you can get out of this unscathed?

You think I will show your little girl mercy — huh?!

Woman
No, no, please, please don't! I don't feel well. It's not what you think. I can explain everything. But leave her alone. Do you hear me?

Phantom
1. You are here of your own free will.
2. You can't just make claims without explaining yourself.
3. I'm only a projection of your unconscious desires.

Woman
Okay. I'll do it.

Phantom
Do what?

Woman
What you said.

Phantom
You mean, you'll keep your promise?

Woman
Yes, yes.

Phantom
Good.

A knock at the door. Turns Dolly and Kenny on, and then off.

Mother
Goodnight, dear.

Woman
Goodnight, mom.

Phantom
Yes, goodnight, mom.

> *Sweeps up the shard of glass into a dustpan,*
> *stands there looking for a place to dispose of them,*
> *then empties the dustpan into the top drawer of the dresser.*

Alright, can we begin?

> **Woman** *nods and snuggles into the bed.*

Phantom
Wonderful.

> *Walks behind the partitioned wall,*
> *and comes out in a smock and glasses,*
> *sits down with a paper pad and pen in hand.*

Alright, dear, let's hear it. A true story from when you were young and scared.

Woman
And my daughter?

Phantom
Shh. We'll get to that after your story.

Woman
But, is she safe?

Phantom
Later!

Woman
What if she's lying there awake and doesn't know where she is or
where I am or how she'll get home?

Phantom
Now your getting tangled up again. And we both know what
happens when you get tangled up…

Woman
Right…

Phantom
Tell me!

Woman
Okay, so when I was young, I was scared of the dark. Well, not
the dark but the noises in the dark. There was this one time
where I heard a sound in the darkness and was petrified.

Phantom
Geez. Try for a little drama. Build it up. Put your heart into it.
Come on, now.

Woman
Okay, okay. There was this noise, this chanting sound. It came
down the hallway, growing louder. It was at my keyhole. It came
under the door right into the room where I was sleeping. It
moved in waves across the floor and made its way into my bed.

Phantom *nods encouraging her to continue.*
What was the sound?

Woman
Fuuu sa sa sa, fuuu sa sa sa…

Phantom *excited.*
Yes. Yes. Yes.

The phone rings.

No!

Woman *answers the phone.*
Hello. Yes. Oh no. She's awake?

I mean. You can't be serious. He can't just…

Let me try.

Hi sweetie. It's mommy. Please don't cry… no, mommy can't come right now… don't cry, darling… no mommy can't come right now because it's too far away… but it'll be morning soon, sweetie, and then we'll see each other… I know… I know… It's dark right now… Please don't cry… Hello? Hello?

Tries calling back several times.
It doesn't work. Begins crying.

Phantom *has taken off the scrubs, and now sits cross-legged on a spiked mat, waiting.*

Now tell me about the darkness.

Woman
But, my daughter...

Phantom
You're doing this for her. Don't you see that? So she'll never feel as alone as she is right now again... this unhappy... this scared.

Woman
I need to comfort her.

Phantom
It's no use. The darkness — come on now — the darkness was...

Woman
The darkness was thick and heavy and stretched out everywhere.

Phantom
Good! Where were you? Show me!

Woman *gets on all fours and begins crawling.*

Phantom
Aha!

Walks after and ties leash around her,
as if she were a dog –
speaks to the audience.

Yes, yes, I know. This is basically breaking the first point, but I have no intention of losing sight of her, that's all.

To Woman.

Say it! Say it now!

Woman *crawling.*
Fuu sa sa sa, fuu sa sa sa – Come to me! Come to me now!

Phantom
Keep going!

Woman
The darkness surrounded me. It entered me. Everything was black, black as soot.

Phantom
Keep going!

Woman *keeps crawling.*

Phantom *continues walking behind her. The oil burner hums, and the lonely sound of a girl crying is heard. Darkness. On a screen a little girl is standing with her back to the audience. Flower petals rain all around her. The camera zooms in, and when she turns around she looks terrible. This clip plays again and again.*

Act II
Scene One

Curtain rises: Duran Duran's "Save a Prayer" fades out.
A humming sound is heard.
The room grows lighter.

Phantom *lays in bed wearing a red silk kimono and slippers, filing nails.*

Woman *crawls around struggling like mad on the treadmill.*

Phantom
The beginning, the beginning, the beginning. The primal scream. The animal within. The endless, gaping darkness.

Woman *continues crawling.*
I can't do this anymore.

Phantom
Funny, that's what Agnes Louise used to say — or, rather what she used to howl. You could hear her wailing from her cave, a keening sound so terrible it pierced the marrow.

Woman *continues crawling.*
I can't do this anymore.

Phantom
Yes, exactly, but with full power, with... with a heart full of pure hopeless fury.

Takes a doll and puts it underneath the kimono.

They used to say that if Agnes Louise howled while a child was brought into the world, the Woman in labor had better try to howl even louder. It was imperative. If she couldn't, the child would be doomed to never know the feeling of... that's not the right phrase, the child would never know how...

Woman
I CAN'T DO THIS ANYMORE!

Phantom *at the same time — pretends to birth the doll, and screams.*
AAAAAAAAAAAAAAAAAAAAAAA!!!!!!!

Woman *stops crawling and falls off the treadmill – a knock sounds at the door.*

Phantom *rolls eyes, turns Dolly and Kenny on, then off, and gives a sign to Woman.*

Woman *panting.*
Goodnight, mom.

Mother
Goodnight, dear.

Phantom *swaddles the doll in the kimono and walks around, rocking it like a baby, making cooing noises.*
This room is inside of you, yes there it is. It is a flowered box, wedged crosswise, trying to find its balance.

Pushed in between your uterus and your sternum, the box lies forever on its edge. And you're there inside it, screaming.

Yes, you are. And even though you're yelling with all of your might, no one can hear you. No one. Your sounds are incomprehensible. Nothing like words.

Not even close.

   Woman *stands to her feet and receives the "little child" that Phantom hands her.*

  Phantom
Here we are, ready to get on with the middle.

   Woman *completely absorbed in the child, she doesn't listen.*

  Phantom
Hey!

   Woman *babbles soothingly at the child, looks happy.*

  Phantom
It's time now, my friend.

    Gently takes the doll from Woman,
     puts it into a drawer.

  Woman
No, please, don't take her.

  Phantom
Hush now. You know it has to be like this.

Woman
But she's so little.

Phantom
And you're so big now.

Woman
I have to be with her.

Phantom
And you have to get away from her.

Woman
But I can't just leave her!

Phantom
You're doing this for her, come on.

Woman
But what if I go too far away and can never find her again?

Phantom
Come on. You can always find something if you want to
find it. You use a metal detector and beep... beep. Or a dog.
There are dogs that can find anything nowadays — drug dogs,
bloodhounds, cadaver dogs.

Woman
Cadavers?

Phantom
Yes, you know. Come on now, stop fussing.

Woman
Do you promise nothing will happen to her?

Phantom
Yes, yes, yes, I may predict, God may strike me down, hocus
pocus filiokus, clothes make the Woman — come, come, come!

Woman *takes Phantom's hand and leads the way. The two
of them walk and walk and walk on a treadmill.*

Phantom *starts talking like a pushy personal trainer.*

Here we go, 1, 2, 3, 4! Come, come, come, come on!

Quickly grows tired and pale.

Are we there yet?

No answer.

It cannot seriously be this far into the middle of the story.

No answer.

You're doing this to get revenge — hmm? Is this about the bottle
thing?

No answer.

I don't even recognize where we are, what is this place?

Woman *stops and points ahead.*

Phantom
Oh, you want to play it like that?

In a stately tone.

What do I behold before me?

Woman
A ravine.

Phantom
Indeed! Do I spy a cave? Is it Agnes Louise's cave? Hey! Hello!
Aggie Lou — are you here? Ha, ha, ha, how rich. Yoohoo —
Aggie Lou! Yes, I just made that up. She's earned a nickname at
least, huh?

Woman
This is where the tidal wave hit.

Phantom
No, of course she isn't here. That was all so long ago, and believe
you me when I tell you how that story ended.

The tidal wave?

A deep hum, reminiscent of the oil burner,
can be heard and felt.

Woman
There are stairs cut into the ravine. Children play there. It's
summertime, everyone is off work, taking it easy.

Phantom
(is listening, but is disturbed by the sound of steel drum music,
which drowns out the humming. Finds two lounge chairs,
unfolds them, and gets comfortable in one of them)

Ah, this is the life, my friend! Come on!

Pats the other chair,
motioning to Woman to lay down, too.

Woman *hesitates.*

Phantom
Come on now.

Woman *reluctantly lies down and tries to sunbathe.*
Attendant arrives with a tray of colorful cocktails with tiny
umbrellas.

Phantom *hides from Attendant behind the lounge chair.*

Attendant *looks at the empty lounge chair next to Woman*
and speaks to her in broken English.

Honeymoon?

Woman *shakes head no.*

Attendant
Ah, girlfriend?

Woman *hesitates then shrugs her shoulders and shakes her*
head, furrows her brow and smiles at Attendant.

Phantom *offended, stands up with arms crossed.*

Attendant *doesn't notice Phantom but looks at Woman just*
a little too long and smiles at her.

Would you like a massage?

Woman
Alright.

>   *Turns on her stomach to let Attendant begin.*

>   **Phantom** *rolls eyes in resignation.*

Geez! Hello... are you there?

Woman
Ah, this is the life, my friend!

>   *The music gets louder and louder.*
>   *Woman and Attendant forget all about Phantom.*

Phantom
What happened?

Woman *voice indifferent.*
With what?

Phantom
The wave!

Woman
The wave?

Phantom
Yes, and the children?

Woman *still indifferent.*
The childr...

>   *Suddenly snaps back to awareness.*

The children!

Stands up so abruptly that Attendant falls backwards.

We're keeping an eye on them. Really. At least now and then. Divide the responsibility between us. A piece for you and a piece for me.

Phantom
And?

Woman *dispirited.*
I… I think I lost my piece.

Phantom
And?

Woman
It all happened so quickly.

Phantom
And?

Woman
I stand up.

Stands and looks at the horizon.

Phantom *also stands up.*
And?

Attendant *stands up too, trying to follow the conversation.*

Woman
I hear laughter and shouts echoing off the mountains and the ravine walls far, far below.

Phantom
And?

Woman
Out to sea, the ocean is a wall. The air is filled with a deep humming. Everything's vibrating.

Phantom
And?!

Woman *curls into the fetal position and holds hands over ears.*
You can hear a rumble in the distance.

Phantom *pulls on her arm.*
This is your moment, your chance to be a hero.

Come on!

Woman
Let me go! I can't do it!

Phantom *shakes her hard.*
Stand up, girl!

Attendant *pushes away Phantom, helps Woman up, makes her look at him and holds eye contact. Slowly starts a huffing, stamping sort of dance, and makes Woman join him.*
Fuu sasa, fuu sa sa, fuu saasa. Fuu sasa, fuu sasa, fuu saasa.

*Sticks out his tongue and beats his chest
and inflates his cheeks.*

Woman *copies Attendant.*
Fuu sasa, fuu sasa, fuu saasa…

Phantom *watches them in alarm, but then joins the
dance, and quickly becomes lost in the rhythm of the words and the
movement.*

Come to me, come to me. Come to me!

The dance grows more wild and more crazed.

Come to me, come to me. Come to me!

Woman *tries to follow Phantom.*

Fuu sasa, fuu sasa, fuu saasa…

The rumble grows louder and louder.

Phantom *stops and looks into the horizon.*
Look, the tide is coming in, foaming and seething!

Woman *stops dead.*

Phantom
Run! Right now. Save them!

Woman *holds onto Phantom's leg.*

Phantom
The wave's coming! It'll smash into them.

Tries to shake off Woman.

Look, there is Hans Jákup. Of course. That old fool. The wave is breathing down his neck. He's clambering for his life... with all the children clinging to him.

Fucking amazing.

Calls out to Hans Jákup.

Hey — did you never hear about equality? She could have done that!

Looks down at Woman.

If she had pulled herself together, that is.

The rumble of the wave fills the room.

Woman *holds on tight. all three of them brace themselves, then silence.*

Phantom *stands up straight trying to look unaffected. turns accusingly toward Woman.*
You're not afraid — you're a coward!

Woman *clings to Phantom.*

Phantom *walks forward for a few feet dragging Woman.*

Yes, yes, yes, you're locked into a gendered arrangement. A pattern of parts. I get it. Your upbringing doesn't exactly inspire heroism. In your world, saviors have a different set of genitals... but bloody hell, girl — shake it off! Come on, come... on!

Woman *continues clinging, shuts her eye.*

Attendant *shakes head, gives up, folds up the lounge chairs and leaves.*

Phantom
Look at me!

Woman *looks up.*

Phantom
Shake it off.

Attempts to shake Woman loose.

Woman
It's too late. No use… This is so pathetic.

Phantom
No. Get up. Stand up. Now.

Pulls Woman up.

Repeat after me: I am here of my own free will.

Woman
I am here of my own free will.

Phantom
I can't just make claims without explaining myself.

Woman
I can't just make claims without explaining myself.

Phantom

And... uhm... I recreate... or, wait... I reproduce my... or... no, look: my subconscious desires are hidden in... make themselves manifest in...

Shit, come on, let's go home.

Tries to take Woman's arm,
but ends up giving her a piggyback ride
walking in the opposite direction.

Scene Two

*Curtain rises: Phantom walks on a treadmill
still carrying Woman.*

Phantom
"The road is long with many a winding turn, that leads us to who
knows where, who knows when, but I'm strong... She ain't heavy,
she's my brother..."

*Puts Woman down. They keep walking, side by side,
without uttering a word for a while.*

Well, how did this all start?

Woman
How? What?

Phantom
How did you make it up?

Woman
Make it up?

Phantom
You need to get to the bottom of this, you know that, right?

Woman
I was there, in the middle of it. There's nothing I could do.

Phantom
I don't really believe this stuff about a wave.

Woman
You don't?

Phantom
It just sounds a little too made up.

Woman
But it happened.

Phantom
To you?

Woman *doesn't answer.*

Phantom
Is this something you yourself experienced? Not so much, huh?

Woman
Some of it.

Phantom
But seriously, that wasn't your story was it? It wasn't your fear?

Woman
No.

Phantom
Maybe you want to stay stuck. Is that it?

Woman
No!

Phantom
Maybe you think it's luxurious to wallow in everything that could
have been, huh, is that it? To shudder deliciously at the thought
of where every worst case scenario might have led you?

Woman
No!

Phantom
The dogs, huh?

Breathes heavily into Woman's face.

The smell of death?

Woman
Stop it!

Phantom
Okay, okay, relax, I'm just saying that it's one thing making things
up. It's another to tell it like it is. That's all I'm saying.

Woman
I didn't make it up. It was there, big and scary, and it came closer,
or, it felt as if it came closer. As if it was something falling on me,
or could have done...

Phantom
And then something on TV scared you as well?

Woman *nods sadly.*

Phantom
Some show?

Woman *nods.*

Phantom
A documentary perhaps?

Woman
Madeleine, that girl who disappeared.

Phantom
Ah, yes. The girl who disappeared while her mom and dad sat outside, drinking wine and eating tapas.

Woman
They just forgot she existed.

Phantom
Unbelievable.

Woman
Horrible.

Phantom
And other shows?

Woman
No... or yes, a movie about Natascha Kampusch.

Phantom
Ah right, that was the one Priklopil locked in his cellar.

Woman
For eight years.

Phantom
Until she was rescued.

Woman
Until she escaped.

Phantom
For God's sake, Woman! What's the point of all this baloney?

Woman
It was just so… It was a really well acted movie.

Phantom
And the tidal wave, where did that come from?

Woman *hesitates sheepishly.*
Grandma.

Phantom
Grandma?

Woman
Yes, it's a true story.

Phantom
So you're telling me that was her worst memory?

Woman *looks away.*

Phantom
And those damn sounds?

Woman *shrugs.*

Phantom
So fuu sa sa sa – it's pure imagination?

Woman
Grandma… grandma was a pretty bad snorer.

Phantom
Incredible! A TV show, a movie, a tall tale, and an old
Woman who snores. Incredible! You really don't have a core to
get to, do you? You just mix up your imagined fear into things
you've seen and heard? Parasitically digest the feelings of others.
Is that it?

> **Woman** *holds her hands over her ears and shuts her eyes.*

Phantom
Tell it like it is.

Woman
The thing about the pieces… that's real.

Phantom
What?

Woman
That I lose my pieces…

Phantom
And by that do you mean your daughter? You lose your girl?

Woman
Yes.

Phantom
What is at the core of that?

Woman

I don't know... maybe I want it to be something that I can... or... something more...

Phantom

More, huh? Always more.

Woman

No... or, I don't know. I just want to know it... I don't want to be one of those people who pretend... yes, even if I might not have felt everything up close and personal... so... just knowing...

Phantom

Oh, darling, you just want to feel a part of the big tragedy that is being human — oh, so lovable.

Woman

Hey, this was your fucking idea!

Pushes Phantom off the treadmill.

Phantom

And your itsy bitsy made-up story.

Woman

You can just get lost.

Phantom

Your pitiful excursion into a void

Woman

Piss off.

Phantom *shakes head, holds Woman off with an open palm, and then leaves.*

Woman *keeps walking, but then stops, understanding that she is now all alone.*

It is quiet, but then a sobbing is heard,
and then a groaning voice takes over:
"You shall search but will find no one.
You will call but no one shall answer you."

Hello?!

Hey, are you here?!

Answer me!

Phantom *walks behind Woman, looks with empathy, and nods sympathetically.*

Woman *notices Phantom.*
Oh, thank God!

Phantom *holds its arms out to embrace Woman.*
Come here, come on.

Woman *clings to Phantom for awhile.*

Phantom
Do you remember your cousin now?

Woman
Yes, she used to scare the daylights out of me…

Phantom *laughs.*
Home?

Woman *nods and tries to act nonchalant.*

Phantom *walks next to Woman, satisfied, humming, until the treadmill stops and they're back in the room again.*

Voila! Your girlhood room.

Scene Three

Curtain rises: the room has changed.
It's dingy and gray.

Woman *lies down on the bed.*

Phantom *tucks her in.*

Woman
My grandmother said that when it happened she felt rooted to
the spot, literally, as if she were something with roots planted
deep into the earth. She said she felt as if she were made of
something heavy, shrunken and silent as a stone, not human. She
said…

Phantom
Hmm.

Woman
She simply couldn't move.

Phantom
Hmm…

Lies down next to Woman in the bed.

Agnes Louise also got stuck. In her cave, there beneath the
bedrock, she got squashed to death. She simply couldn't stop
growing. She bowed her head, hunched over and tried to make
herself small. But as she grew, her shoulders and back pressed
into the sharp rock. It cut into her flesh. When she died, they
didn't even try to retrieve her body. They just left her there. That
poor gargantuan girl left all alone in death.

      Woman *puts her hands over her ears and climbs under the*
bed.

Phantom
And so her cave of refuge became her tomb. Poor Agnes Louise.
And the poor villagers — the stench was appalling. That big body
rotting away. That takes time, I'll tell you. A brain that big and
mushy. An ass that wide.

      Woman
Please stop!

      Phantom *drags Woman by one foot from beneath the bed.*
People said that one of her feet stuck out of the cave entrance,
tall as a full grown oak. And the colors of her carcasse were a
thing to behold, a work of art — meat-red and pus-yellow, flesh
weeping off the bone, melting like a Salvador Dali painting, until
the joints began to show, chalk white in the sunlight. And the
birds feasted. Their caws and croaks kept the villagers awake at
night. Graaaa. Graaaa.

      Woman *pulls her leg free of Phantom's grip and stands.*
Stop!

Phantom
Legend has it that when the wind blew just right you would
breathe Agnes Louise into you. And I don't just mean the

rancid smell of her. As her rotting body moldered, little pieces blew away and coated everything like a film. If you opened your mouth, even a little bit, you would taste her on your tongue.

> *A warm wind blows onto the stage*
> *and through the audience.*

Woman
Ugh. Disgusting!

> *Gags.*

Phantom
People said it wasn't that bad. A mix of citrus, seaberries, and red currant. The texture was crunchy like a pop rock, you know that powder you stick on a lollipop and lick it.

> **Woman** *pulls the duvet over her head to hide.*

> **Phantom** *sticks out tongue, tastes, shrugs.*
A pack of lies, every bit of it. Probably.

> *Sits down, yawns, curls up at the foot of the bed,*
> *falls asleep muttering.*

Your girlhood room exists. All these little things. The flowers entwined in your thoughts...

> *The room grows gloomy and quiet,*
> *the flowers on the wallpaper wither,*
> *and the petals fall.*

Scene Four

Curtain rises: The room grows brighter.
Songbirds sing, a rooster crows.

Woman *wakes up, stretches, and changes from pajamas into*
street clothes, walks around the room humming and straightening up
this and that and tidying the dolls.

Phantom *wakes up and watches Woman.*
You're in a good mood.

Woman
It'll be light soon and then I'll be off.

She turns the music on. A knock sounds at the door.
She turns the music off.

Mother
Good morning, dear.

Woman
Good morning, mom.

Mother
Are you coming downstairs? Breakfast is ready.

Woman
I'll be down in a minute.

Mother
Is everything alright?

Woman
Everything's fine, mom.

Sits and begins to apply makeup.

Phantom *walks around her, expectantly.*
Beginning, middle, and…

Woman
End. Yes, yes, I know.

Phantom
But?

Woman
Haven't I said enough already?

Phantom
So you're just going to leave without knowing how it could end?

Woman
What do you mean could end.

Phantom
Nothing is preordained. You know that, right?

Woman
I know what I want. That's what I know.

Phantom
Darling.

A girl's room heralds new ways of thinking. It is a research lab, an experimental space.

Here it is possible to cut, examine, burn away, preserve in formaldehyde.

This is where needs are found, where desire is invented. This is where the future is created.

Woman
But I know what my future is. It is her. It's my girl. It is to make sure she's never unhappy again.

Phantom
My, oh my, something's crunching between my teeth.

*Picks up the doll, starts picking teeth,
occasionally licking fingers clean.*

What's this on my tongue: Yum, red currant carcass, citrus corpse. Pop, pop. Can you taste it?

Woman *tries to wrestle away the doll. Phantom stops her.
The phone rings. Woman quickly picks up. Phantom fidgets with the
doll as Woman speaks.*

You're an asshole.

Sweetheart, I'm sorry. Mommy didn't know it was you. Are you okay? Where's daddy? Let mommy talk to him.

Waits.

Are you an idiot or something?

Yeah, it went just like I told you it would. She was scared out of her mind. And you, you weren't there. I couldn't even get hold of you.

No, don't put me on speaker. Do you hear me?

Hi, hello, sweetie — yes, mommy is so excited to see you in your dress. Yes, I'll be there soon, very soon. Okay, bye, bye... but, mommy needs to talk to daddy again – hello?! Hello!

> **Phantom** *continues to fidget with the doll, "accidentally" breaks one of the arms off.*

Oops!

Woman
Give me that.

> *As she reaches out to take the doll,*
> *she realizes she has also lost an arm,*
> *the same one as the doll.*

Give her to me now.

> **Phantom** *yanks on one of the doll's legs.*

> **Woman** *loses footing, howls in pain.*

Phantom
Sit down!

Woman
Give her to me, please!

Phantom
Sit. Down.

The oil burner starts up again.

Woman *sits down at the table.*

Phantom *walks over to the dresser and takes a glass jar full of formaldehyde out of the bottom drawer, puts it on the table in front of Woman and unscrews the lid, then drops the doll's arm into the liquid.*

There. Now I'm ready to hear the end of the story.

Woman *shakes head and trembles.*

Phantom
Are you not feeling well, dear?

Puts a hand against Woman's forehead.

Woman *trembles violently, looks frightened, holds herself with her one arm, tries catching her breath.*

Phantom
But dear, you're as cold as ice!

Starts dressing Woman in clothing: scarves, woolen socks, hats, a coat.

There, that's better.

Woman
I'll never be rid of you, will I?

Phantom
Now you're just being nasty. Also, you look like a bag lady.

Woman
I never should have left her. I never should have come.

Phantom
Tangled. Tangled. Tangled…

Woman
Who… what are you?

Phantom
Me? I am… the rabbit with the pocket watch, tick tock, tick tock… or maybe I know how to fly…

Woman
Why are you here? What do you want with me?

Phantom
Come morning, I'll wing across the sun-dappled sea, and I'll find her before she forgets that she's mommy's little girl.

Woman
Like hell you will!

Phantom
…and then I'll gently take her in my arms…

Woman
I don't believe you.

Phantom
And she'll live happily ever…

Woman
You're lying!

Phantom
And you're ruining the coherence of your story.

Woman
There is no coherence!

Phantom *pulls the doll's hair hard.*

Woman *screams and jerks her head back as if someone is pulling her hair. A knock is at the door, and behind it rustling and clinking can be heard. The oil burner stops.*

Mom?

No answer.

Mom?

Phantom
Hush now.

*Gets up, dropping the doll on the table
to look behind the door.*

Woman *head hits the table like the doll's. She sits up trembling and scared.*

Phantom *comes back in with a tray of breakfast and puts it on the table in front of Woman.*

Breakfast is served. Now... about that ending.

Woman *shakes head.*

Phantom
You know this has to stop, don't you?

Woman *looks away.*

Phantom
A girl's room is a freezer.

Here slabs of butchered thought harden in the cold. But there's also some beauty in it. Freezer burn sparkling on dead hopes. Rime cracks. Joy is iced over. In the end, the cold dulls everything. Just wait.

Woman *tries to cover her ears but only has one hand.*

Phantom
Come now, eat.

Shakes the doll threateningly.

Eat. Now.

Woman *slowly starts forcing herself to eat.*

Phantom
There you go! Yes, have some more. That's it.

Satisfied, turns on Dolly and Kenny. A knock sounds. Phantom looks around confused. Another knock sounds as Woman bumps her knife against the table.

What's wrong?

Woman
Isn't this enough?

Phantom
You can't eat anymore?

Woman *shakes head.*

Phantom
Shall we make a final binding contract then?

Woman
What do you mean?

Phantom
You finish your meal and I'll finish telling you her story?

Woman
Whose story?

Phantom
Agnes Louise's of course, silly.

Woman *decisively pushes the jar of formaldehyde toward Phantom.*

Phantom
Later. Eat. Listen.

Woman *stuffs bread into her mouth.*

Phantom
Agnes Louise rotted away. The rain washed the ooze of her innards to the river.

Woman *gags.*

Phantom
Come now, it wasn't as bad as all that. She was swept into the stream, became a part of the water cycle. People said the fishing was never better than it was that year. One might say that Agnes Louise's final contribution was as fertilizer for the ocean bed. All the sea creatures got a good slurp of her.

Woman *puts down her food and holds a hand over her mouth.*

Phantom
Okay, okay, I take your point. Years passed. Times grew hard. You know what it was like back then: no fish, boats capsizing, empty shelves in the stores, et cetera, et cetera. It was in such a year that a girl went to tend the cows and had to shelter from a downpour. Can you guess what cave she found to hide in? Bingo — that's right, the one with Agnes Louise's skeleton.

Eat! Eat!

Woman *tries to eat, crunching at a bit of toast.*

Phantom *sets the doll down on the table.*

Of course she knew about her, had grown up with stories of poor Agnes Louise, who took up too much space in her Mother's house and had to cross the mountains to find a place to be in this world.

Her overgrown femurs looked like marble pillars, her skull the curved roof of a temple. Oh, the beauty, oh, the wasted life – no, just kidding, that wasn't what the girl was thinking at all. She was practical and sensible —bless her.

The very next day, she went and hauled off a kneecap, got it to roll down the slope, and it didn't take long for the villagers to crush most of the right leg into a powder to use as fertilizer. No one had ever seen plants grow like this: grain, root, berry shrub, herb.

    Woman *removes one thing at a time — hats, scarves — eats more enthusiastically while listening.*

    Phantom
But the best part is still to come.

    Woman
What?

*   The phone rings.*
*   She looks at it but doesn't pick it up.*

    Phantom *looks at Woman in surprise, motions to turn off the phone.*

    Woman *nods.*
So what was the best part?

    Phantom
Her back.

    Woman
Her back?

    Phantom
Well her back and chest cavity. The sunken vertebrae of a girl, who had crouched around her loneliness, and the white cage where her ribs had held her sorrow.

Woman
What did they use it for?

Picks at the shell off of a soft boiled egg,
but struggles using just one hand.

Phantom
Out of these... these rows of vertebrae and her sternum...

Can't help but assist Woman
in picking the shell off the egg.

... and what driftwood they collected...they...

Feeds Woman with a spoon.

Woman *swallows and takes the spoon – eats, and grows impatient.*
They did what?

Phantom
They built a ship, of course, a schooner so stout and seaworthy, she could sail to the world's end and back, main mast and jib, white sails furled.

Woman *smiles agreeably.*
And they called it...

Phantom *can't stand to look at Woman making a mess of the egg, unscrews the lid from the jar of formaldehyde, dries off the doll's arm and sticks it back onto the doll.*

That's right. Of course they called her The Agnes Louise.

Plunks down the doll on the deck of the model schooner,
and pleadingly looks at Woman.

Woman *slowly returns her arm to visibility and she sits for*
a while, but then looks at Phantom, smiling.

Phantom
What?

Woman *stands up and walks toward Phantom.*

Phantom *backs away.*

Woman *walks right up to Phantom and puts her arms*
around it, holding it tight and burying her face in its chest.

Phantom *stands there, amazed, then hugs Woman back.*

Woman
A girl's room is a battlefield.

Phantom
And a sanctuary.

"Take My Breath Away" by Berlin plays
and they dance close together. When a moment has passed,
the situation becomes embarrassing,
and they let each other go.

Woman
Can I go now?

Phantom
Yes, yes, go.

Woman *fussily packs.*

Phantom *sits down to eat the rest of the breakfast. Gets something in between its teeth and uses a hair pin as a toothpick.*

Woman *finally ready to go, waves.*

Phantom *waves with the hair pin in its hand. Stops, when Woman has left. Looks at the hair pin, at the doll, and out at the spectators with a smile. Turns off the music. Stands up with the hair pin in one hand and a glass of juice in the other. Walks over to the dresser. Puts the glass down, opens the top drawer a bit, pulls out a mortar and pestle, puts pieces of glass from the drawer into it, crushes them, pours them into the juice, stirs it with the hair pin. All while singing with the melody of "The Moment I Wake up".*

You're going, you're going, but where do you think you're going?
You're going, you're going, but where do you think you're going?
You're going, you're going, but where do you think you're going?
Where do you think you are you are goooiiing?

Looks at the glass, grimaces, but downs it.

Woman *far off.*
I can't do this anymore!

Phantom *in American accent.*
Amen. Amen.

About *A Girl's Room*

A Girl's Room allows us to step into and be completely surrounded by the imagined privacy of a room of one's own. Polyphonic and at times manic, the adult enters the girl's childhood room and is haunted by the voice of her mother and her own youth. She is all ages at the same time; the voice of cultural mythologies becoming her final oppressor.

This work dissolves the boundaries and thresholds that exist between the stages of the self: in development, in conflict, in confusion – paradoxical, contradictory and at times harmonious – all at the same time. A girl's room and the acclimated girl become the overcoming force in these works, a being that learns to refuse to be reprimanded or put in place.

The Karma Goat, the matching literary pair of *A Girl's Room*, is also published by IPI Press.

Marjun Syderbø Kjelnæs (born 1974) is a well-known and active voice on the Faroese literary and dramatic scene, and she has published a wide range of works since her debut in 2000. Her first novel, *Skriva í Sandin*, 2010 (Skriv i sandet, Viatone 2013, translated into Danish by Hugin Eide) received the Nordic Children's Book Prize in 2011. *The White Raven* appeared in 2011, and her latest youth novel *Sum Rótskot* was nominated for the Nordic Council's children's and youth literature prize in 2021. She has received a number of prizes and grants, and her works have been translated into the Nordic languages as well as English, French and German.

Gentukamarid and *Karmageitin* were both nominated for the 2023 Nordic Council Literature Prize.